THIS BOOK IS DEDICATED TO ALL OF
THE WOMEN AND GIRLS OUT THERE.

THIS BOOK BELONGS TO THE BEAUTIFUL,

_____

You, my love, are beautiful.
Just the way you are.

Did you know that your body is capable of doing so many incredible things?

Your senses – touch, taste, smell, sight, and sound – rely entirely on your body!

Your body tells you when you are sick and does EVERYTHING it can to help you get over that sickness!

You, my love, are so unique.
Not one other person is
exactly like YOU.

unique

being the only one of its kind; unlike anything else.

Your body is there whenever you need it.

Your body helps store your memories!

Your body lets you love others. Your body lets you care for others.

Your body lets you cry, laugh, smile, and feel all of the emotions.

Repeat after me, "Other opinions of my body, DO NOT affect or involve me."

Did you know that every second, your body produces 25 million new cells? That means in 15 seconds, you will have produced more cells than there are people in the United States.

Sometimes, we get sad because our bodies don't look like other people we admire....

....but that is because we are all beautiful in different ways.

Your weight does not determine your worth.

If we all ate the same, did the same activities, and dressed the same....

We would still all look different, but beautiful.

My love, YOU are enough.

All bodies, are good bodies!

"It doesn't have anything to do with how the world perceives you. What matters is what you see."

◂◂◂ ◂◂◂◂ ◂ ◂◂◂ ◂◂◂ ◂◂◂◂ ◂

Gabourey Sidibe

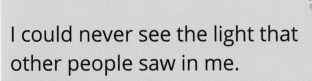

About the Author:

My name is Margaret and I am the owner of Mountain Rose & Co. My entire adult life, I have struggled with body dysmorphia.

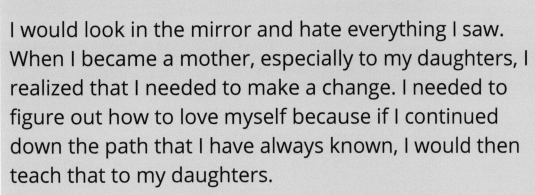

I could never see the light that other people saw in me.

I would look in the mirror and hate everything I saw. When I became a mother, especially to my daughters, I realized that I needed to make a change. I needed to figure out how to love myself because if I continued down the path that I have always known, I would then teach that to my daughters.

This was when I started my journey on becoming body positive. It's not an easy journey, but it is worth it. I hope this book helps you in the way it helped me. Please reach out if you ever need anything.

Printed in Great Britain
by Amazon

17233435R00016